DATE DUE			
A-2			
MAY 19 1998			
G- OCT 19 1998			
637			

AWESOME ATHLETES

EMMITT SMITH

Paul Joseph
ABDO & Daughters

Published by Abdo & Daughters, 4940 Viking Drive, Suite 622, Edina, Minnesota 55435.

Copyright © 1997 by Abdo Consulting Group, Inc., Pentagon Tower, P.O. Box 36036, Minneapolis, Minnesota 55435 USA. International copyrights reserved in all countries. No part of this book may be reproduced in any form without written permission from the publisher.

Printed in the United States.

Cover and Interior Photo credits: Wide World Photos
Allsport USA

Edited by Kal Gronvall

Library of Congress Cataloging-in-Publication Data

Joseph, Paul, 1970-
Emmitt Smith / Paul Joseph.
        p. cm. — (Awesome athletes)
Includes index.
Summary: A brief biography of the Dallas Cowboys running back who has earned such titles as Rookie of the Year and Super Bowl Most Valuable Player in his first five years in professional football.
ISBN 1-56239-640-4
l. Smith, Emmitt, 1969- --Juvenile literature. 2. Football players—United States—Biography—Juvenile literature. 3. Dallas Cowboys (Football team)—Juvenile literature. [1. Smith, Emmitt, 1969- . 2. Football players. 3. Afro-Americans—Biography.]
I. Title. II. Series.
GV939.S635J67 1997
796.332'092—dc20
[B]   96-8385
                                                                          CIP
                                                                          AC

Contents

Smooth Cowboy

Believe it or not, 16 **professional** football teams passed on Emmitt Smith when choosing their **draft** picks. Emmitt, they claimed, was either too small, too slow, or just not strong enough to make it in the hard-hitting **National Football League (NFL)**. How wrong they were!

The Dallas Cowboys chose Emmitt with the 17th pick in the 1990 NFL draft. In his **rookie** season, Emmitt started the second game. He ended the season with 937 yards, offensive Rookie of the Year honors, and a trip to the Pro Bowl—pro football's All-Star Game.

In his next five seasons, Emmitt collected four NFL **rushing** titles, three **Super Bowl** titles, the league's **Most Valuable Player (MVP)** Award, a Super Bowl MVP Award, and was chosen for the Pro Bowl each year.

Let's not forget that the year before Emmitt arrived, the Cowboys had won only one game the entire season. Emmitt made 16 other teams look pretty foolish for not drafting him when they had the chance.

Dallas Cowboy running back Emmitt Smith.

Early Years

Emmitt worked hard all of his life to get to be where he is. It did not happen overnight. He not only worked hard at football, but he also worked hard at school to be the best student he could be.

Emmitt J. Smith was born May 15, 1969, in Pensacola, Florida. His father, also named Emmitt, was a bus driver, and his mother, Mary, worked in a bank. Emmitt has three brothers (Erik, Emory, and Emil) and two sisters (Marsha and Connie). They were a very close family with a firm set of **values**.

When he was very young, people knew that Emmitt was a gifted athlete. By the age of five he was playing tackle football with children much older, and was easily better than them all.

At seven he began playing organized tackle football in a local league. People were very impressed by his running style and the way he could avoid tacklers.

By the time Emmitt had reached high school, people around town were already talking about him.

Emmitt Smith at the University of Florida.

High School Sensation

Emmitt made the **varsity** squad when he was only a freshman at Escambia High School. In four years, Emmitt led his team to a 42-7 **record**. Escambia also won two Florida State Championships.

Even more, Emmitt averaged more than 2,000 yards **rushing** per season, finishing with 8,804 yards in his high school career. Only one other high school player rushed for more yards than Emmitt did, and that happened more than 40 years ago.

Emmitt ran for at least 100 yards in every game in his junior and senior years. In one game he ran for more than 300 yards!

Emmitt could have set the high school record for most career rushing yards, but in most games he didn't play the fourth quarter. The team was so far ahead that

Emmitt was taken out. Emmitt didn't get upset when he was taken out. He would be on the sidelines cheering his team on—louder than anyone.

Emmitt wasn't just playing football during this time. He studied hard and got good grades. He also visited the **White House** where he participated in the "Just Say No to Drugs" campaign. Emmitt never tried drugs and he also avoided gangs, even though he grew up in a rough neighborhood. His dream was to go to college and be a student-athlete. He knew that the only way that his dream would come true would be if he worked hard on the field and in the classroom.

Too Slow?!

After a great high school career on the field as well as in the classroom, it was time for college. You would think that Emmitt could go to any school he wanted. But that was not the case. College football **scouts** doubted his ability, believing he was too slow. One scouting service didn't even name him as one of the top 50 high school running backs.

It didn't take long for Emmitt to prove his **critics** wrong. He decided to stay close to home for college, choosing the University of Florida in nearby Gainesville.

By the third game of his freshman season he was the starting running back. It was a nationally televised game against Alabama. And in his first college start Emmitt set a Florida **record** with 224 yards on 39 carries!

That was just the start of a great college career. In 25 of his 34 games at the University of Florida, he rushed for 100 yards or more. In one game he ran for 316 yards.

In just three years he rushed for 3,929 yards, breaking Neal Anderson's career **rushing** record at Florida.

Emmitt Smith carries the ball for the University of Florida.

Too Small?!

After playing three years in college, Emmitt decided he would try the NFL. Although school meant a lot to him, he knew that football was now his number one **priority**. He left college early to enter the NFL **draft**.

Despite Emmitt's accomplishments in high school and college, NFL **scouts** were saying he was too slow and too small for the NFL.

The Dallas Cowboys had other ideas. The year before they drafted Emmitt, they were the worst team in the league, only winning one game. But Dallas head coach Jimmy Johnson had his eye on Emmitt. They had a great, young quarterback in Troy Aikman, and now they needed a great running back.

Coach Johnson and the Cowboys took no chances. They **traded** to get the 17th pick in the draft, and they chose Emmitt. Sixteen other teams believed what the scouts had to say about Emmitt, and passed on him.

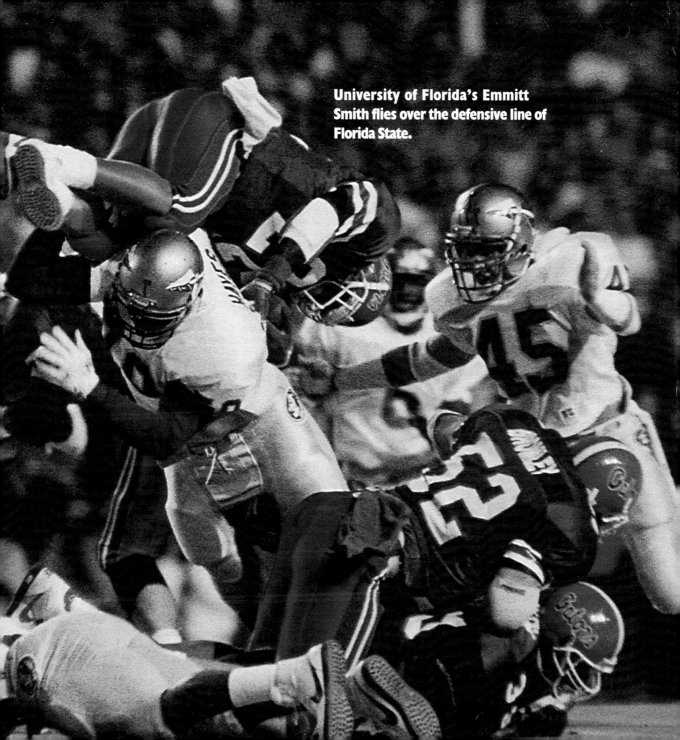

University of Florida's Emmitt Smith flies over the defensive line of Florida State.

Emmitt missed **training camp** and the first game because he didn't think that the Cowboys were offering him a fair **contract**. After they worked out the final contract, he started in the second game of his **rookie** season.

Emmitt had a great rookie year, finishing the season with 937 yards **rushing**, 11 touchdowns, and Offensive Rookie of the Year honors.

Emmitt Smith (22) carries the ball into the end zone against the Giants.

Too Weak?!

But the **critics** didn't stop. They were now saying that Emmitt was taking too many hits, and because he was too small, he wouldn't be able to last in the NFL without getting injured. But Emmitt didn't stop either. And he never listened to those critics.

In only his second season, Emmitt became the best running back in the NFL. He led the league in **rushing** with 1,563 yards and scored 13 touchdowns. More important, he helped the Cowboys reach the playoffs. The Cowboys beat the Bears in the first round, with Emmitt running for more than 100 yards. Unfortunately, the Cowboys lost the following week to the Detroit Lions.

Despite the playoff loss, it had been a great season. Only two years earlier, the Cowboys had won only one game. Now they were on their way to the top of the league with the help of their great running back.

Emmitt Smith (22) heads toward open field against the Cardinals.

Emmitt hugs his counterpart, Thurman Thomas, after the Cowboys' victory in Super Bowl XXVII.

THE MAKING OF AN AWESOME ATHLETE

Emmitt Smith (top) during his days at the University of Florida.

1969	1976	1986	1987
Born May 15 in Pensacola, Florida.	Plays mini-mite football for the Salvation Army Optimists League.	At Escambia High School in Pensacola, Florida, Smith runs for 8,804 yards and scores 106 touchdowns.	At the University of Florida in Gainesville, Smith establishes 58 school records in 3 seasons.

How Awesome Is He?

With three NFL rushing titles in his first five seasons, Smith joined an elite group of NFL running backs. Compare his first five years with the first five seasons of these great backs:

Eric Dickerson	8,256 yards	(1983-87)
Emmitt Smith	**7,183 yards**	**(1990-94)**
Walter Payton	6,890 yards	(1975-79)
Jim Brown	6,463 yards	(1957-61)
Tony Dorsett	6,270 yards	(1977-81)
Franco Harris	5,133 yards	(1972-76)

EMMITT SMITH

TEAM: DALLAS COWBOYS
NUMBER: 22
POSITION: RUNNING BACK
HEIGHT: 5 FEET 9 INCHES
WEIGHT: 209 LBS.

1990	**1993**	**1994**	**1995**	**1996**
First round draft choice of the Dallas Cowboys.	Wins NFL's MVP Award and leads the Cowboys to a Super Bowl win over the Buffalo Bills, 52-17.	Named MVP as Cowboys defeat the Buffalo Bills in the Super Bowl, 30-13.	Sets NFL single-season record with 25 touchdowns.	Leads Cowboys to victory over the Pittsburgh Steelers in the Super Bowl.

- 1990 NFL Rookie of the Year
- 1993 NFL MVP
- 3-Time Super Bowl Champ
- 4-Time NFL Rushing Champ
- 6-Time Pro Bowl Selection
- 1994 Super Bowl MVP
- 1995 NFL TD Leader

Highlights

Back-to-Back

In 1992, the Cowboys and Emmitt made it all the way to the top. They showed everyone that the Cowboys were the best team in the NFL, and that Emmitt was the best running back in the league.

Emmitt became the first player since Eric Dickerson to lead the league in **rushing** in back-to-back seasons, finishing with 1,713 yards.

But Emmitt did one other thing: he helped lead his team to the **Super Bowl**. The Cowboys finished with a 13-3 regular-season **record**. In the playoffs, they crushed the Philadelphia Eagles, and then beat the San Francisco 49ers in a close game to advance to the Super Bowl. In both games Emmitt rushed for more than 100 yards.

In the Super Bowl the Cowboys destroyed the Buffalo Bills 52-17. Emmitt ran for 108 yards and a touchdown.

The Cowboys and Emmitt were now the best. What more could they accomplish?

Emmitt Smith wins the MVP Award for his performance in Super Bowl XXVIII.

Back-to-Back Again

In 1993 it got even better. Emmitt went back-to-back-to-back, winning his third-straight **rushing** title. And he helped lead the Cowboys to back-to-back **Super Bowl** titles.

The Cowboys walked through the regular season and the playoffs, where they again met the Buffalo Bills in the Super Bowl.

Nothing much had changed in one year, as the Cowboys again dominated the Bills, winning the Super Bowl 30-13. Emmitt ran for 132 yards and scored 2 touchdowns. And no one was surprised when he won the Super Bowl **MVP** Award.

To top off a great year, Emmitt was named MVP of the entire **National Football League**.

In 1994, the Cowboys came close to winning three-straight Super Bowls. Barry Switzer took over as head coach, and the winning continued. They made it to within

one game of the Super Bowl before losing to San Francisco in the NFC Championship game.

Emmitt continued to burn up the turf, finishing the year with 1,484 yards, third best in the league.

Emmitt Smith crashes through the Steeler defense.

They're Back

In 1995, the Cowboys and Emmitt returned to greatness. They won their third **Super Bowl** in four years, beating the Pittsburgh Steelers in a hard-fought game. Emmitt had two touchdowns, which gave him five career Super Bowl touchdowns—a new **record**.

Emmitt's regular season is what led the Cowboys to their Super Bowl win. He again won the **rushing** title, his fourth in five years, with 1,773 yards. He is only the fifth running back in league history with three-or-more 1,500-yard seasons. And he was the touchdown leader for the second year in a row with 25.

Opposite page: Emmitt Smith waves to the fans after another Super Bowl victory.

Too Unbelievable

Emmitt has accomplished both team and personal goals. At only 27 years old and in only 6 years in the league, he has easily done more than 99 percent of all NFL players—past and present.

When asked if there was anything else he wanted to accomplish, Emmitt responded, "I would like to win more **Super Bowls**, more **rushing** titles, and go back and finish my **degree** at college." He has already accomplished one of his goals. On May 4, 1996, Emmitt graduated from college. After taking classes during the off-season for the last six years, Emmitt graduated. His family was indeed proud of him.

For a person who was too small, too slow, and not strong enough to play college or pro football, he truly showed the world that with hard work he could be the best.

"I know I'm not the fastest guy around," said Emmitt, "and I know I'm not the strongest guy either. It doesn't bother me at all. Because I have determination and I work harder, and most of all I get the job done."

Former Cowboys' coach Jimmy Johnson and Emmitt Smith celebrating their NFC Championship.

GLOSSARY

contract - A legal document signed by a player that states how much money they will get paid and how many years they will play for a particular team.

critics - People who look for the weaknesses in others.

degree - Something you earn after completion of meeting all of the requirements in college.

draft - An event held in April where NFL teams choose college players. The worst team gets the first pick.

Most Valuable Player (MVP) - An award given to the best player in the league or Super Bowl.

National Football League (NFL) - A professional football league in the United States consisting of a National and American Conference, each with 15 teams.

priority - Having more importance than something else.

Pro Bowl - An All-Star game played at the end of the season in Hawaii. The best players at their position get to play.

professional - Playing a sport and getting paid for it.

record - The best that has ever been done in a certain event.

rookie - A first-year player in the NFL.

rushing - To run with the football.

scouts - The people that watch athletes play football and determine if they have what it takes to make it at a higher level.

Super Bowl - The NFL championship game played between the American and National conference champions.

trade - Exchanging something (a player, draft pick, or money) to get something else.

training camp - Where football players go for a certain amount of time before the season starts to get in shape, both physically and mentally.

values - Something that a person or family holds dear and believes in strongly, such as religion, education, and family.

varsity - The best team in high school.

White House - The building where the President of the United States and his family lives. Also where the President's administration works.

Index